Understanding Your Baby's Milestone Moment

A Practical Guide to Nurturing Growth and Skills During Key Developmental Stages for Your Infant's Progress from 7 to 10 Months

Adegboye S. Aduragbemi

INTRODUCTION

Welcome to a thrilling new phase in your baby's development and discovery journey! A critical developmental stage for your child occurs between the ages of 7 and 10 months, marked by increased mobility, growing curiosity, and developing independence.

We are excited to offer you a thorough guide to comprehending and supporting your baby's development during this exciting infancy stage in this book. Every chapter focuses on answering common questions and concerns parents may have regarding their baby's growth and well-being, from their growing physical and developing language skills to their blossoming social interactions and emotional connections.

When your baby starts to crawl, cruise, and explore their environment with greater assurance, you might have to deal with many unfamiliar situations and difficulties. We are here to support you every step of the way with helpful advice, professional insights, and evidence-based strategies, whether you are introducing new foods, creating sleep routines, or encouraging your child's increasing independence.

This book is jam-packed with advice, ideas, and materials to help you be a more capable parent and commemorate the exciting turning points in your exploring adventurer's life. Our mission is to support you as you journey through this exciting transition into parenthood with self-assurance, joy, and a profound understanding of the miracles of your child's growth.

Chapter One

The physical development phases of newborns

How can I aid in my infant's physical growth at this point?

You can promote physical development by giving your infant lots of opportunities for supervised tummy time, crawling, standing up, and cruising along furniture. Provide toys and items that promote the development of reaching, grasping, and fine motor abilities.

What physical growth milestones might my kid hit between 7 and 10 months?

Your baby may reach developmental milestones between the ages of 7 and 10 months, including sitting up on their own, rolling over or crawling, standing up, cruising around furniture, and potentially even taking their first steps.

How can I get my baby to begin rolling over?

A secure and open area for exploration, appealing toys or objects placed just out of reach to stimulate mobility, and lots of praise and encouragement for their efforts are all excellent ways to help your baby begin to crawl.

When can I anticipate my infant standing up on their own?

Although the exact time can vary, most newborns start pulling up to stand between 7 and 10 months. You may encourage their attempts by putting strong furniture or objects within reach for your infant to grip onto and practice standing.

What should I do if my infant is not meeting physical milestones in the anticipated amount of time?

Continue to provide practice and exploration opportunities for your infant if they are not meeting physical milestones within the anticipated timeframe. If you have concerns about their development, speak with your pediatrician. If necessary, early intervention services could be suggested.

How can I ensure my infant is in a secure setting to explore and grow physically?

By childproofing your home, securing gadgets and furniture to avoid tipping or accidents, and eliminating small objects or choking risks from your baby's reach, you can make sure their surroundings are safe. During playtime, keep a watchful eye on the kids and be aware of any potential risks.

Should I be worried if my baby isn't crawling or pulling up to stand yet?

Babies often take different amounts of time to attain milestones, like pushing themselves to stand and crawling. Talk to your pediatrician for more assessment and advice if you are worried about your child's physical development.

What are some physical development exercises I can perform with my baby?

Supervised tummy time, rolling a ball back and forth, encouraging crawling or scooting with alluring toys, practicing sitting up and standing with assistance, and using toys that stimulate reaching and grasping are some activities that aid in developing physical skills.

How can I support my infant in developing their fine motor skills at this stage?

Giving your baby toys with various textures, forms, and sizes to handle, nesting or stacking toys to help with hand-eye coordination, and finger foods to practice self-feeding can enhance their infant's fine motor skills.

What part does my baby's physical development play while we play outside?

Your baby will benefit greatly from outside playtime as they explore various surfaces, textures, and settings, practice gross motor skills like crawling or walking on grass, and receive sensory stimulation from the sun, wind, and other natural sounds.

How can I support my infant with their coordination and balance at this point?

By giving your infant the chance to try sitting on their own, standing with assistance, and eventually taking little steps while holding onto your hands or furniture, you may help them develop their balance and coordination. Providing them with sturdy toys and objects to grip can also help them grow more robust muscles and better balance.

What are some telltale signals that my child is prepared to begin independently standing or walking?

When your baby is comfortable pulling up to stand, cruises smoothly along furniture, takes steps while hanging onto your hands or furniture, and shows interest in exploring their environment while standing, those are indications that they may be ready to start standing or walking independently.

How can I give my infant a secure space to practice standing and cruising?

By removing potential hazards like sharp edges or unstable furniture, fastening heavy objects that could topple over, and providing solid surfaces for them to grip onto, like low tables or ottomans, you can create a secure space for your baby to practice standing and walking.

What should I do if my infant appears reluctant or afraid to try new physical activities?

If your child appears reluctant or afraid to undertake new physical activities, give them lots of support and encouragement, divide tasks into smaller, more manageable steps, and give them encouragement and praise for their accomplishments.

Should I be concerned if my infant would rather crawl than walk at this age?

Babies often discover that crawling is a more effective way to get around than walking, especially if they have mastered the skill. For further assessment, go to your pediatrician if you worry about your baby's development or mobility.

How can I help my kid improve their ability to use objects and hand-eye coordination?

To facilitate your baby's exploration and manipulation, offer a variety of toys and objects with diverse sizes, shapes, and textures, practice reaching and grasping exercises together, and participate in interactive play that involves passing objects back and forth. You can support your baby's development of hand-eye coordination and manipulation skills.

What effect does exercise have on my baby's general growth and health?

Due to its capacity to improve bone density, cardiovascular health, muscle strength, and coordination, physical activity is essential for your baby's overall development and health. Encouragement of movement and active playtime benefits children's physical health and develops a lifetime love of exercise.

How can I support my baby's posture and movement by helping them to build strong core muscles?

By allowing your baby to have tummy time, which encourages them to raise their head and chest off the ground, and by involving them in activities that demand that they sit upright and maintain balance, like playing with toys while sitting unsupported or sitting on a stability ball, you can aid in the development of your baby's core muscles.

What should I do if my child has a minor mishap or falls while engaging in physical play?

If your child has a minor fall or mishap while engaging in physical play, soothe and reassure them, look for any indications of harm or discomfort, and provide first aid if required. When you see any changes in your behavior or range of motion, it could be a sign of a more severe injury. If necessary, get medical help.

How can I balance other everyday obligations with ensuring my infant receives enough exercise?

You can make sure your baby receives enough exercise by introducing quick bursts of energetic play throughout the day, such as tummy time, crawling races, and dancing to music. Keep your infant occupied and active, and balance structured and unstructured playing.

The developmental trajectory of infants

What is the recommended weight gain for my infant during this time?

Babies usually acquire 1.5 to 2 pounds each month during this stage, though individual development rates may differ. If you are worried about your infant gaining too much weight, speak with your pediatrician.

What are some telltale signs that the baby is developing typically?

A consistent increase in weight, length, or height and the accomplishment of developmental milestones like sitting up on their own, crawling, and standing up on their own are all indicators of proper growth.

How can I make sure my child is eating enough food to thrive?

Ensure your infant gets enough nutrients by providing a range of nutrient-dense meals, such as iron-fortified cereals, fruits, vegetables, protein sources, breast milk or formula, and healthy fats. Regularly observe your baby's growth and development and adhere to your pediatrician's feeding recommendations.

If I am worried that my baby isn't developing as they should, what should I do?

If you're worried about your child's growth, get an evaluation from your pediatrician. Your baby's development trajectory, food intake, and general health can all be assessed by your pediatrician to see whether more testing or care is required.

How can I monitor my baby's development at home?

You may monitor their development at home by periodically measuring your baby's length or height, weighing them with a baby scale, and recording their growth metrics over time. You may track your baby's growth trajectory by plotting their measurements on growth charts.

What part does exercise play in the growth and development of my infant?

Exercise helps maintain healthy growth and development by enhancing bone density, muscle strength, and motor function. Promote tummy time, floor play under supervision, and opportunities for active mobility and exploration for your infant.

If my baby's growth percentile shifts, should I worry?

The growth percentiles of newborns typically vary throughout time. While a shift in the growth percentile does not always portend trouble, monitoring your child's general growth trajectory is vital, and speaking with your pediatrician if you have any concerns is critical.

How can I encourage a diet rich in nutrients while guarding against giving too little or too much?

By providing balanced meals and snacks, letting your child self-regulate how much food they eat, and honoring their hunger and fullness cues, you can help them develop healthy eating habits. Do not use food as a reward or punishment for your infant or exert pressure on them to eat.

What can affect my baby's development and growth at this point?

Genetics, dietary habits, general health, the environment, and the availability of stimulating and supportive caregiving environments might affect a child's growth and development.

Creating a loving and stimulating environment can support the best possible growth and development.

When will my baby's development rate stop being as rapid?
Growth rates in babies usually decrease after the first year of life. Compared to infancy, growth usually happens more steadily and slowly during toddlerhood.

What are some telltale signals that my kid is going through a growth spurt at this point?
An increase in appetite can identify a growth spurt, longer nursing sessions or more frequent feedings, fussiness or clinginess, rapid weight gain, or quick body lengthening.

How can I encourage play and engagement to help my kid grow and develop?
You can support their growth and development through play and connection by giving your infant age-appropriate toys and activities that promote exploration, sensory stimulation, and the progress of gross and fine motor skills.

What part does sleep play in the development of my infant?
Since sleep is when growth hormone is predominantly secreted, getting enough sleep is crucial for average growth and development. Implementing effective sleep patterns and

maintaining a consistent bedtime schedule guarantees your child sufficient rest.

How can I make my baby's environment stimulating so that it grows and develops?

Several toys, books, and sensory experiences should be available to create a stimulating atmosphere. Opportunities for safe exploration and active play should also be provided, as should interactive activities that support social, emotional, and cognitive development.

Should I be concerned if my infant's growth appears to be slowing down or plateauing?

It is not unusual for growth to temporarily plateau or slow down, particularly following a period of fast growth. However, you should get evaluated by your pediatrician if you observe a notable or sustained departure from your baby's regular growth track.

What are some things that might influence my baby's hunger and the amount of food consumed at this point?

The discomfort of teething, sickness, schedule adjustments, and increased mobility and activity can all impact your baby's appetite and nutrient intake. Provide a range of wholesome foods, exercise patience, and pay attention to your infant's indications.

How can I get my infant to sample different foods and flavors?

By providing a range of flavors, textures, and colors, setting an example of healthy eating habits, and letting your child explore and experiment with food quickly, you may encourage your baby to try new foods and flavors.

What signals indicate that my child is prepared for solid foods?

When children are ready for solid foods, they should be able to sit up on their own, show interest in what they are eating, reach for food or objects during meals, and no longer have the tongue-thrust reflex.

Should I be concerned if my baby's growth percentile is consistently higher or lower than usual?

Growth diversity among individuals is typical, even though growth percentiles can offer helpful information. If there are notable variations from your baby's growth curve or if you have concerns about their growth, speak with your pediatrician.

If my child is formula- or breastfed, how can I make sure they are getting enough nutrients?

If your baby is being breastfed or formula-fed, ensure they are getting enough nourishment by feeding them frequently, adhering to your pediatrician's feeding guidelines, and routinely checking their growth and development.

How babies develop in terms of their ability to move around and explore

What is the normal progression of my baby's mobility at this stage?

Babies frequently reach important mobility milestones between the ages of 7 and 10 months, including learning to sit on their own, crawling, standing up on their own, and cruising on furniture or other surfaces.

Which indicators indicate that my child is prepared to begin crawling?

Your baby may be getting ready to crawl when they push up on their hands and knees, rock back and forth, and exhibit increasing curiosity by reaching for objects that are out of reach.

How can I help my infant start to crawl?

Promote the development of crawling in infants by providing ample practice opportunities, such as putting toys just out of reach to get them moving, setting up a secure and open area for them to explore, and gently encouraging and supporting them while they crawl.

If, after ten months, my infant still isn't crawling, should I be worried?

Though the start of crawling might occur at any time between 7 and 10 months, it usually does. You may not need to worry if your kid is meeting other developmental goals and hasn't begun to crawl by the time they are ten months old. However, if you have any particular worries, speak with your pediatrician.

What are some safe strategies for encouraging movement and exploration?

Provide a range of age-appropriate toys and objects for your baby to explore, babyproof your home to eliminate any risks, and keep a close eye on your child during playtime to encourage safe exploration and movement.

How can I help my kid with their gross motor skills at this stage of development?

Give your infant many opportunities to practice sitting, crawling, standing, and cruising. You can also foster the development of gross motor skills by providing toys and activities that require reaching, gripping, and manipulating objects.

When can I anticipate my child standing up independently and moving about furniture?

Most newborns begin pulling themselves to stand between eight and ten months and cruising along furniture. Ensure everything is secure and safe to encourage your baby's exploration and mobility.

What are some telltale signals that my child is prepared to begin standing independently?

When your baby can stand on their own without much assistance, bears weight on their legs while clinging to furniture, and has greater assurance in their balance and coordination, those are indications that they may be ready to start standing on their own.

How can I help my infant stand on their own?

Encourage your baby to stand independently by giving them a low, vigorous surface or piece of furniture to grip onto and praising and supporting their efforts while they practice standing and balancing.

What part does exploration play in the whole development of my baby?

Your baby's general development dramatically benefits from exploration since it allows them to learn about their surroundings, improve their coordination and spatial awareness, and develop problem-solving abilities via trial and error.

Which indicators indicate that my child is prepared to begin crawling?

When your baby is ready to try rolling over on all fours, they should also be scooting or shuffling on their tummy, displaying increased upper body strength, and displaying interest in objects just out of reach.

How can I get my baby to begin rolling over?

Provide lots of tummy time, put toys just out of reach to stimulate reaching and gripping, and create a safe environment that promotes movement and discovery to help your child start crawling.

If my infant starts walking instead of crawling, what should I do?

Babies frequently forego crawling and begin walking right away. When your child begins to demonstrate walking skills, such as standing up and cruising along furniture, encourage them and give them opportunities for safe practice.

What safety measures should I take as my kid gets more mobile?

Childproofing your home involves locking up furniture, covering outlets, blocking staircases with safety gates, and removing potential choke dangers, such as small items, from the environment.

How can I help my kid develop their fine motor skills now?

Provide toys and items that promote grabbing, reaching, and manipulating, including stacking rings, blocks, and shape sorters, to aid in developing fine motor skills. Give your infant lots of time to explore and learn.

When can I anticipate my child to begin standing up on their own?

Babies usually begin pulling themselves up to stand between the ages of eight and ten months. Please encourage your child to reach this milestone by giving them low surfaces or sturdy furniture to help them stand up on.

What are some strategies for encouraging my child to look around them?

Create a secure, engaging space for your infant to walk about freely and explore various surfaces, objects, and textures to promote discovery. Keep a close eye on things and offer assistance if needed.

How can I use play to encourage the development of gross motor skills?

By providing toys and activities that stimulate crawling, cruising, and walking—such as ride-on toys, push toys, and soft play mats for crawling and rolling, It is possible to foster the growth of enormous motor abilities via play.

Should I be concerned if my infant looks less eager to explore or more cautious?

In terms of their physical development, newborns typically develop at their own rate. As your baby explores and makes their way through their surroundings, support and reassure them. Encourage their efforts.

What part does exercise play in my baby's general growth and development?

Exercise enhances confidence, strength, and coordination and promotes emotional and cognitive growth. As the day goes on, encourage movement and vigorous play to help your baby's general health and wellbeing.

Growth tracking phases and issues about infant development

How can I monitor my baby's development and growth at home?

Using the growth charts your pediatrician has provided, you can track your baby's weight, length, and head circumference to monitor their progress at home. Furthermore, pay attention to your baby's developmental milestones, including their motor abilities, language acquisition, and social interactions, to ensure they reach age-appropriate milestones.

What are some indicators that my child is maturing and growing as it should?

Consistent weight gain, advancement in motor abilities (such as rolling, sitting, and crawling), greater chattering and vocalization, and social contact (such as smiling and responding to names) indicate your baby is growing and developing as it should.

What should I do if I'm worried about the development or growth of my child?

Talk to your pediatrician if you have any worries regarding the growth or development of your child. To ascertain whether more evaluation or intervention is required, your pediatrician can perform a comprehensive review that includes a physical examination and developmental assessments.

What warning indicators or red flags could point to a developmental delay or cause concern?

Significant delays in meeting developmental milestones, loss of previously learned skills, ongoing difficulty with feeding or swallowing, restricted eye contact or social interactions, and odd or repetitive behaviors are red flags or warning signs that may point to a developmental delay or cause concern.

How frequently should I plan well-child visits with my pediatrician to keep an eye on the development and growth of my child?

During the first year of life, well-child checkups with your pediatrician are usually planned at regular intervals, such as every two to three months. During these appointments, your child's physician may monitor your child's growth, development, and general health and answer any worries or queries you may have.

How can I help my baby grow and develop healthily?

Make sure your baby gets enough nutrition to support healthy growth and development. It includes breast milk or formula for babies and a range of age-appropriate solid meals as they get used to eating solids. Offer abundant chances for exercise, entertainment, and discovery, and participate in caring conversations to bolster their social and mental growth.

Should I be worried if my baby's development percentile on the growth chart varies over time?

As a baby grows and develops, it is normal for their growth percentile to vary significantly over time. But, to ensure your child is growing at a healthy rate, your pediatrician may need to do additional testing if there are noticeable changes in the growth percentile.

What part does genetics play in the growth and development of my child?

Your baby's growth and development, including aspects like height, weight, and body proportions, are influenced mainly by genetics. While some aspects of growth are influenced by genetics, environmental variables, diet, and general health are all important in promoting the best possible growth and development.

When should I start to worry if my kid is gaining or losing weight?

See your pediatrician if your infant constantly falls or rises beyond the projected growth curve on the growth chart or if you see any noticeable changes in their weight gain or decrease. Your baby's overall health and nutritional state can be evaluated by your physician, who can advise on proper feeding and growth tracking.

What can I do if my kid has specific medical issues or health concerns to promote their growth and development?

Collaborate carefully with your doctor and other specialists providing treatment for your child if they have any unique health issues or medical problems that could affect their growth and development. To enhance your infant's general health and wellness, adhere to prescribed treatment regimens, therapies, and interventions.

What typical developmental milestones should my child hit at this point?

Typical developmental milestones between seven and ten months of age include better hand-eye coordination for gripping objects, babbling or uttering short phrases, and beginning to show preferences for particular foods and textures.

How can I monitor my child's growth at home between visits to the pediatrician?

Using a baby scale, you can measure your baby's weight regularly, record any changes in their length or height, and watch for their developmental milestones to monitor their growth at home. Share your observations with your pediatrician by keeping a growth notebook or using a growth monitoring app.

What are some possible influences on my baby's growth and development now?

During this stage of development, several factors can impact your baby's growth and development, including genetics, diet, general health, environmental stimulation, and opportunities for socialization and exploration. Creating a caring and stimulating environment can positively impact your baby's growth and development.

At this stage, should I be concerned if my baby's development rate slows or plateaus?

During this phase, a baby's growth rate may occasionally slow or plateau, especially when they become more active and explore their surroundings. But for more assessment and direction, If you have concerns about your child's development, it's essential to consult with a pediatrician.

What indicators indicate my child might not receive enough calories or nourishment to thrive?

Indications that your child could not receive enough calories or nourishment for healthy growth include lethargy or low energy, fussiness or irritability, delayed development, and slow weight increase or loss. If you're worried about your baby's eating habits or nutritional intake, speak with your pediatrician.

How can I help my infant develop healthy eating habits and dietary preferences during this period?

Providing a range of nutrient-dense meals in various textures and flavors promotes whole grain, fruit, vegetable, and lean protein consumption, and you can foster healthy dietary habits and preferences. Let your infant explore and feed themselves with finger foods to promote independence and good eating habits.

What should I do if my baby's growth curve suddenly and significantly changes?

Your baby's development curve may alter suddenly or significantly. See your pediatrician to find out what could be causing the change. Your physician can advise additional testing, imaging investigations, and blood tests to exclude any possible medical conditions or dietary deficiencies.

Can I use online tools or growth charts to monitor my baby's development and growth?

Indeed, there are many growth charts and resources accessible on the internet, encompassing standardized growth charts sourced from reputable entities such as the CDC and the WHO, both widely regarded as thought leaders in the field. You can use these charts to monitor your baby's growth and assess how it compares to typical growth trends for the child's age and gender.

What part do exercise and physical activity play in helping my baby grow and develop healthily?

Exercise and bodily activity are essential for your baby's healthy growth and development because they build muscle, enhance balance and coordination, and maintain general physical health. To promote physical development, provide opportunities for play and movement that are safe and supervised.

When should I consult a doctor if I'm worried about my baby's development or growth?

You should consult a doctor if you have any worries about your baby's growth or development—such as delayed developmental milestones, sluggish weight gain, or strange symptoms or behaviors. Your pediatrician can perform a comprehensive assessment and propose tailored guidance and assistance according to your child's specific requirements.

How infants develop in terms of parenting and support stages

How can I encourage my child's increasing independence while giving them the required direction and oversight? You can encourage your baby's increasing independence by providing opportunities for exploration and self-directed play in a secure and supervised setting. Give your kid the freedom to explore their newfound talents while offering assistance and encouragement when needed.

2. What are some practical methods for easing my baby's separation anxiety and encouraging a strong bond between us? Healthy attachment and separation anxiety can be effectively managed by adhering to regular routines, providing lots of physical affection and comfort, and progressively introducing brief separations interspersed with reunions. When you have to be apart from your baby, give them a comfortable or transitional item, and make sure you say goodbye before you go.

3. how can I create and preserve a caring and responsive caregiver relationship with my baby during this stage? A loving and responsive relationship between caregiver and child can be built and maintained by paying attention to your baby's needs and cues, acting on their signals quickly and affectionately, and showing them regular attention. To develop

a strong emotional attachment, engage in interactive play, snuggling, and verbal conversation.

4. How does positive discipline help to mold my baby's behavior and promote a healthy growth pattern? By establishing firm boundaries, modeling positive behavior, and using gentle advice and redirection instead of punishment, positive discipline plays a critical role in influencing your baby's behavior and promoting healthy growth. For positive actions, give encouragement and praise; for undesirable behaviors, give mild reprimand.

5. How can I use meaningful play and interactions to help my baby's social and emotional development? Playing peekaboo, reading books together, and mimicking your baby's sounds and movements are examples of responsive and reciprocal activities that can help promote your baby's social and emotional development. Provide socialization opportunities to encourage social skills and empathy in children and other caregivers.

What are some strategies to help my infant with language development and communication skills at this stage? Regular discussions with your infant, using essential words and phrases, reacting to their vocalizations, and identifying items and behaviors in their surroundings will all help promote language development and communication abilities. To encourage language learning and understanding, read aloud from books, sing along to songs, and describe everyday activities.

How can I create an environment that is kind and helpful for my baby's cognitive development and problem-solving abilities?

By offering your infant age-appropriate toys and activities that promote exploration, manipulation, and discovery, you can generate a loving and supportive atmosphere to support their cognitive development and problem-solving abilities. Give your infant the chance to explore their senses by allowing them to play with various textures and materials. As they explore and learn, give them gentle supervision and encouragement.

What are some practical methods for handling typical parenting issues like feeding or sleep disruptions?

Establishing a regular bedtime routine to encourage sound sleep habits, providing consolation and assurance during nighttime awakenings, and seeking support from healthcare providers or lactation consultants for feeding difficulties or concerns are all effective strategies for managing common parenting challenges.

How can I take care of myself first and balance my needs as a parent and taking care of my child?

Make self-care a priority by establishing reasonable goals, asking for help from friends and family, and scheduling time for things that give you back energy and general well-being. Recognize that taking care of yourself helps you to better care for your child and practice self-compassion.

When should I look for more help or resources to help me with my parenting difficulties?

If parenting gives you stress or overwhelm, or you're unsure how to meet your baby's requirements, look for further help or resources. Consult reputable medical professionals, parenting support groups, or internet sites for direction, inspiration, and practical tactics.

How can I provide a fascinating and safe environment for my kid to explore and be curious?

Create a secure and engaging space for your infant with developmentally appropriate toys, books, and activities to foster their curiosity and discovery. As your baby plays independently and discovers new things, let them explore various textures, colors, and sounds, but keep a watchful eye on them.

What are some methods for encouraging my baby to bond and engage positively with other family members or caregivers?

Encourage shared activities like games, story reading, and strolls to help your infant develop healthy connections and a strong bond with other family members or caretakers. To foster a sense of security and trust, emphasize the significance of responsive caregiving and gentle handling.

How can I help my infant develop coping mechanisms and emotional resilience during stressful or transitional times?

By creating a stable, loving environment for your child, offering consolation and assurance during stressful situations or times of change, and modeling healthy coping mechanisms like deep breathing or pausing when feeling overwhelmed, you may help your child develop emotional resilience and coping abilities.

What are some strategies to help my baby develop sound sleep patterns and pleasant connections with sleep?

Create a peaceful, distraction-free sleep environment, stick to a regular bedtime schedule, and respond quickly to your baby's sleepy cues to help them develop strong sleep associations and habits. Help your infant develop self-soothing abilities by gradually training them to go to sleep on their own.

How can I identify my baby's unique temperament and personality and react accordingly?

You may identify and address your baby's unique temperament and personality traits by paying attention to your baby's behavioral indicators and preferences, such as activity level, adaptability, and sensitivity to stimuli. To suit your baby's particular requirements and preferences, modify how you provide care.

How does responsive feeding contribute to my baby's health and nutritional needs?

Responsive feeding is essential to promoting their general well-being and nutritional needs by enabling your infant to control their hunger and intake. To encourage healthy eating habits, provide breast milk or formula on demand and swiftly attend to signs of hunger and fullness.

How can I use play and exploration to support my baby's physical development and motor skills?

You can support their motor development and physical skills by giving your child opportunities for active play and exploration, such as supervised tummy time, crawling over obstacles, and reaching for objects of interest. Provide toys and equipment that are age-appropriate and promote coordination and movement.

What are some practical methods for handling and lowering worry and tension in parents at this early stage of infancy?

Parental stress and anxiety can be effectively managed by engaging in self-care activities like mindfulness training, relaxation techniques, and physical activity, asking friends and family for social support, and, if necessary, seeking professional counseling or therapy.

During this period of infancy, how can I foster a co-parenting relationship with my partner that is both good and supportive?

Foster a cooperative and upbeat co-parenting dynamic with your spouse by being transparent about your parenting objectives, duties, and worries and working together to make decisions and solve difficulties. Put your partner's efforts in raising your child first by prioritizing quality time together and communicating your gratitude and admiration.

What are some telltale signals that my baby is growing and maturing well?

Consistent growth and weight gain, meeting developmental milestones on schedule or with minor deviations, exhibiting curiosity and involvement in their surroundings, and creating safe bonds with caregivers indicate that your baby is flourishing and developing healthily and pleasantly.

Chapter Two

The phases of cognitive development

How do babies' 7–10-month cognitive development milestones progress?

During this phase, infants' cognitive development accelerates as they get more inquisitive, investigate their environment, and gain a deeper comprehension of cause-and-effect relationships.

What cognitive milestones might my baby accomplish between 7 and 10 months old?

Improved object permanence (realizing that items persist even when out of sight), an extended attention span, starting to mimic noises and behaviors, and exhibiting problem-solving abilities are some of the cognitive milestones that may occur at this stage.

How can I help my infant at this stage of cognitive development?

You may boost their cognitive development by offering your infant a range of toys with diverse textures, shapes, and sounds, participating in interactive play and conversation, and promoting exploration and problem-solving.

What are some telltale signs that my infant is developing object permanence and a heightened awareness of their surroundings?

Your baby may react to familiar people or objects even when out of sight, explore for concealed objects, show increasing curiosity about their surroundings, and be more aware of their surroundings as they acquire object permanence.

How can I support my infant's exploration and curiosity at this age?

You can foster their curiosity and exploration by introducing new situations and experiences, allowing your baby to engage in hands-on play with safe items and toys, and giving them lots of praise and encouragement for their achievements.

What part do interactive games and playtime play in the development of cognition?

In addition to helping with thinking outside the box and solving problems, playtime, and interactive activities are essential for cognitive development because they encourage language development through engagement and communication with caregivers.

What easy activities can I do with my infant to encourage brain development?

Playing basic games like "pancake" or "Where's your nose?" and providing toys that stimulate sorting, stacking, and nesting are easy ways to foster cognitive development. Other simple activities include playing peekaboo to emphasize object permanence.

How can I support my infant in strengthening their recall and memory?

By frequently repeating routines and activities, giving consistent cues and prompts, and providing opportunities for practice and repetition, you can aid in your baby's development of memory and recall skills.

What is the best time to read aloud to your infant, and what are the benefits to their cognitive development?

You can start reading to your infant as early as infancy and incorporate it into your daily routine. Reading to your infant helps them acquire new words and ideas, develops their language skills, and cultivates a love of learning.

What should I do if my kid appears to be easily distracted or has a short attention span?

Try to reduce distractions during playtime, offer activities in short, manageable portions, and give your infant lots of positive reinforcement for focused attention and engagement if they seem easily distracted or have a short attention span.

What part does imitation play in this stage of my baby's cognitive development?

Your baby's cognitive development is greatly influenced by imitation as they start to watch and imitate the actions and behaviors of others. Promote imitation by showing your infant how to do basic gestures like waving or clapping and rewarding them when they copy you.

How can I support my infant in learning to solve problems at this age?

By giving your infant toys with secret compartments, nesting cups or blocks to investigate, and age-appropriate puzzles, you can encourage the development of problem-solving abilities. When your infant has difficulties, please encourage them to try new things and provide them with gentle assistance.

How can I encourage my infant to be curious and creative when they are playing?

Introduce open-ended toys that promote experimentation and exploration, such as shape sorters, stacking rings, and blocks, to your infant to spark their creativity and wonder. To stimulate their senses, provide a range of materials with various textures, hues, and sounds.

How can I support my baby's language development as they develop cognitively?

Talking to your infant often, explaining your everyday activities, and reacting to their coos, babbling, and communication efforts will all help promote language development. Language learning is also aided by reading aloud, singing songs, and reciting nursery rhymes.

What are some indicators that my child is starting to grasp fundamental cause-and-effect relationships?

Reaching for items, shaking or banging toys to make noises, and repeating activities that result in a desired outcome—like dropping a toy to watch it fall—are indications that your baby is starting to comprehend cause-and-effect relationships.

How can I encourage sensory exploration in my infant to help with cognitive development?

Provide your infant the chance to touch, taste, smell, hear, and see a range of materials and items to aid in their sensory exploration and cognitive development. In sensory bins, provide safe objects for tactile inquiry, such as pasta, rice, or textured fabrics.

What are some strategies for integrating education into my baby's daily activities?

Name items and describe their properties during play, involve your baby in home chores like sorting laundry or stacking containers, and promote observation and exploration during outings and nature walks to integrate learning into daily activities.

How can I encourage my infant to play cooperatively with others at this age?

To promote cooperative play, set up playdates with other infants or toddlers, give your child chances to socialize with siblings or other children, and set an example of good social skills by sharing and taking turns when playing.

What part does repetition play in the cognitive development of my infant?

Repetition is essential to your baby's cognitive development to form brain connections, improve memory, and reinforce learning. Repetition of enjoyable hobbies, music, and games might aid in your baby's cognitive development.

How can I help my baby's cognitive development at home by setting up a stimulating environment?

You may create a stimulating atmosphere by providing a range of age-appropriate materials and toys, changing out toys frequently to keep them interesting, and creating secure areas for indoor and outdoor exploration and discovery.

The sensory and cognitive development of infants

How do babies' seven-to-ten-month sensory development progress?

During this phase, babies' sensory development advances as they hone their senses of sight, hearing, touch, taste, and smell. They also become more skilled at processing and interpreting sensory data from their surroundings.

What are some telltale markers of growing sensory ability in my baby?

Developing sensory talents include a desire to explore objects through touch, an enhanced attention span in response to familiar sounds, the ability to track moving objects with the eyes, and preferences for specific food textures and flavors.

How can I use regular activities to help my baby's sensory development?

By giving a range of age-appropriate toys and objects with various textures, shapes, colors, and sounds for exploration, participating in sensory-rich activities like messy play or water play, and exposing your baby to a variety of sensory stimuli in their surroundings, you can support your baby's sensory development.

What part does sensory exploration play in the maturation of cognition?

Sensory exploration supports cognitive development in infants by giving babies valuable sensory input that strengthens brain connections and helps them learn about their surroundings and make sense of the world. It helps them develop cognitive abilities like memory, attention, and problem-solving.

How can I support my infant's playtime cognitive development?

By giving your baby toys and activities that encourage exploration, problem-solving, and imitation, participating in interactive play and games that pique their curiosity and creativity, and giving them opportunities to practice new abilities and concepts, you can support cognitive development during playtime.

What typical cognitive milestones might my baby meet between seven and ten months?

Improved object permanence (realizing that objects exist even when they are out of sight), a greater capacity for imitation of actions and gestures, the start of understanding fundamental cause-and-effect relationships, and the ability to solve problems, such as figuring out how to get to a desired toy, are typical cognitive milestones during this stage.

How might regular interactions help my baby's cognitive development?

By talking to your infant frequently, describing your actions and the environment around them, giving them opportunities for exploration and problem-solving, and partaking in activities that promote imitation, memory, and attention, you may support cognitive development through regular interactions.

What are some strategies for using sensory experiences to support language development?

Encourage your baby to vocalize and react to the sensory input by using rich, descriptive language to describe the textures and sounds of chirping birds, for example, and by defining other sensory stimuli your baby is experiencing. It will help to promote language development through sensory experiences.

How do I avoid overstimulation if I restrict my sensory experiences?

Offering your kid a range of sensory experiences in moderation helps promote healthy sensory development without overwhelming or overstimulating them, even though it's crucial to be aware of their unique sensory demands and preferences.

How can I tell if my infant has difficulties or sensitivities to certain types of stimuli?

Avoiding particular textures or sensations, getting easily overwhelmed by sensory input, exhibiting uneasiness or distress in reaction to bright lights or loud noises, and exhibiting strange behaviors during sensory encounters are all possible indicators of sensory sensitivities or problems. Confer with a developmental specialist or your pediatrician if you have concerns regarding the sensory development of your infant.

How can I support my infant's sensory play exploration of various textures?

You can promote their discovery of various textures by offering your infant a range of safe and developmentally appropriate materials to touch, manipulate, and explore, including fabric swatches, soft and rough objects, smooth and bumpy surfaces, and objects with intriguing tactile features.

What are some strategies for integrating sensory experiences into regular tasks and routines?

By introducing sensory-rich aspects like textured bath toys during bathtime, serving a range of meals with diverse tastes and textures during mealtimes, and creating chances for outdoor exploration and sensory play in nature, you may integrate sensory experiences into everyday routines.

What benefits can sensory play offer my infant's general development?

Playing with toys stimulates their senses and helps your baby learn to use their fine and gross motor skills, improve cognitive skills like creativity and problem-solving, control their emotions, interact with others, and communicate.

Which sensory activities are available for me to do at home with my baby?

Creating sensory bottles with colorful liquids and objects, playing with sensory bins filled with rice, beans, or water beads, finger painting with edible paint that is safe to eat, and using fabric squares or sensory books to explore various textures are a few examples of sensory activities.

How can I encourage sensory exploration in my infant to help with cognitive development?

By giving your infant a chance to play freely and solve problems, encouraging them to use their senses to investigate and engage with their surroundings, and providing them with age-appropriate toys and activities that pique their curiosity and imagination, you can support cognitive development through sensory exploration.

How does my baby's ability to learn and digest information relate to sensory integration?

The brain's capacity to arrange and interpret sensory information from the surroundings is known as sensory integration. Your baby's capacity to learn, pay attention, control their emotions, and participate in meaningful interactions with their environment is enhanced by effective sensory integration.

How can I make my baby's house a sensory-friendly place?

You can create a sensory-friendly environment by offering a range of sensory-rich materials and experiences, reducing exposure to loud noises and visual distractions, ensuring safe and comfortable areas for play and exploration, and providing opportunities for sensory stimulation throughout the house.

Are there any red flags I should know about regarding my infant's sensory development?

Extreme sensitivity or aversion to specific sensory stimuli, problems paying attention or self-regulating, delayed developmental milestones, and ongoing difficulties eating, sleeping, or interacting with others are all potential warning indicators of sensory issues. Are you concerned about your child's sensory development? Consult your pediatrician or a developmental specialist.

How can I modify sensory activities to meet my baby's unique requirements and preferences?

By paying attention to your baby's reactions and preferences, providing options and choices that align with their interests, modifying the duration or intensity of sensory experiences as necessary, and showing concern for their comfort and well-being, you can alter sensory activities to suit their needs.

What are the advantages of playing with my baby's senses?

The development of creativity and imagination, stimulation of brain growth and neural connections, improvement of fine and gross motor skills, support for emotional control and social interaction, and promotion of sensory exploration and discovery are all advantages of sensory play.

Baby's mental development

How can I encourage my infant's brain growth at this time?

Provide your infant with stimulating toys and activities that promote problem-solving, exploration, and sensory stimulation to help facilitate their brain development. Talk to your infant often, describe your actions, and acknowledge and react to their cues and motions.

What are some telltale signals that my child is becoming adept at solving problems?
Trying to reach for things that are just out of reach, playing with different toy play ideas, and demonstrating perseverance in completing a task are indications that one is developing problem-solving skills.

How can I support my infant's exploration and curiosity?
Encourage your baby to explore and be curious by giving them access to a range of age-appropriate toys and objects, safe, supervised opportunities to explore their environment, and letting them handle and feel different things and textures.

What part does memory play in the mental development of my infant?
Your baby's ability to recall familiar faces, locations, and routines and draw lessons from the past is a crucial part of brain development. Promote memory formation by implementing regular and consistent daily routines and activities.

How can I help my infant at this stage develop language skills?

Talking to your baby frequently, using straightforward, repeated language, identifying objects and movements, and enthusiastically and encouragingly reacting to their communication attempts all support your baby's developing language skills.

What are some strategies for helping my child develop early literacy skills?

Please encourage your child to read at an early age by reading aloud to them regularly, pointing out words and pictures in books, singing nursery rhymes and songs, and allowing them to handle and explore books and other reading materials.

How can I help my infant play imaginatively?

Give your infant plenty of unstructured playtime to explore and create with their imagination. Open-ended toys and materials like blocks, dolls, and dress-up outfits are great ways to encourage imaginative play.

What are the telltale indicators that my child is becoming aware of the permanence of objects?

Seeking for hidden items, realizing that objects exist even when out of sight, and expressing surprise or happiness when they reappear are indications of developing object permanence.

How can I help my infant as they learn about cause and effect?

Provide toys and activities that let your baby press buttons, turn knobs, and manipulate things to elicit a reaction to encourage cause-and-effect learning. You may also promote cause-and-effect learning by verbally narrating the relationships between the objects throughout daily activities.

Should I worry if my kid seems quieter or perceptive than other babies?

Infants grow at their own rate and might have very different temperaments. Encourage your baby's efforts and provide them opportunities for social engagement and stimulation if they seem more reserved or wise, but also honor their need for privacy and quiet observation.

What are some strategies for helping my child develop early math skills?

Playtime activities that involve counting, sorting, and matching, such as matching shapes or items, sorting toys by color or size, and counting blocks, can help develop early numeracy skills.

How can I foster my child's imagination and creativity?

You can foster their imagination and inventiveness by allowing your child to play freely with art supplies like crayons, paints, and play dough and explore and try various textures and mediums.

What part does socialization play in the mental development of my infant?

Social connection facilitates language acquisition, emotional control, and perspective-taking, all critical components of mental growth. Promote social connection by organizing playdates, family get-togethers, and conversations with classmates and caregivers.

How can I aid with my infant's emotional growth at this point?

Encourage your baby's emotional development by attending to their signs and signals immediately and sensitively, ensuring they are in a secure and supportive setting, and providing techniques to calm themselves and manage their emotions.

What are some indicators that my infant is starting to follow basic directions and instructions?

When your baby responds to their name, follows simple motions like waving or pointing, and shows understanding through actions or replies, these are indications that they are starting to understand simple instructions or directions.

How can I foster my infant's feeling of self-governance and independence?

Allowing your baby to make simple decisions, like choosing between two toys or food, and giving them opportunities for self-directed play and exploration in a secure and supervised environment will help foster independence and autonomy.

What part does playtime play in the mental development of my baby?

Playtime is essential for learning and growth because it offers chances for social contact, creativity, problem-solving, and sensory exploration. Promote various engaging play activities to aid your infant's brain growth.

How can I facilitate a seamless transition for my infant between activities?

Give your baby gentle cues and routines to help them transition between activities seamlessly. Some of these routines include humming a song or offering a comforting object. You should also give them time to adjust and transition at their own pace.

What are some strategies for helping my infant develop resilience and coping mechanisms?

By creating a safe and encouraging atmosphere, demonstrating healthy coping mechanisms like deep breathing or self-soothing techniques, and providing consolation and comfort during stressful or uncertain moments, you can encourage resilience and coping abilities.

When should I bring my worries regarding my baby's mental development to the attention of a healthcare professional?

If your worries are related to your baby's mental development and include things like chronic behavioral or emotional problems that interfere with day-to-day functioning, regression in previously learned skills, or noticeable delays in meeting developmental milestones, get in touch with a healthcare provider.

Chapter Three

The social and emotional development phases of infants

How do infants' social and emotional development evolve during the months of seven and ten?

As infants grow aware of their caretakers and environment, form bonds, show a spectrum of emotions, and start interacting socially with others, their social and emotional development advances.

What social milestones might my kids accomplish when they are seven or ten months old?

Social milestones at this period could include starting to play simple games like peekaboo, displaying separation anxiety when not with caretakers, smiling and laughing in response to social interactions, and demonstrating interest in other people.

How can I help my infant at this period of social development?

By giving your infant lots of chances for healthy social interactions with peers, siblings, and caregivers, as well as by immediately and warmly reacting to their signs and signals, you may help your baby develop social skills.

What are some telltale indicators that my child is developing ties and attachments to caregivers?

While your baby shows signs of discomfort while separated from key caregivers, seeks comfort and reassurance from familiar individuals, and exhibits joy or excitement upon reunion, these are all indicators that your baby is developing attachments and relationships with caregivers.

During this phase, how can I support my infant in overcoming separation anxiety?

By maintaining a consistent schedule, giving your child lots of comfort and assurance before and after separations, and progressively lengthening the time spent apart while maintaining a nurturing and encouraging atmosphere, you may assist your baby in overcoming separation anxiety.

What part does my baby's social and emotional development play when they play with their caregivers?

Your baby's social and emotional development greatly benefits from playtime with caregivers because it fosters bonding, trust-building, and the acquisition of critical social skills like sharing, cooperating, and taking turns.

How can I encourage my infant to play interactively with others at this age?

Playdates with other infants or toddlers, opportunities for cooperative play (such as rolling a ball back and forth or using interactive toys), and modeling desirable social behaviors during interactions are all ways to promote interactive play.

What are some techniques to support my infant in expressing and controlling their emotions?

Offering your baby age-appropriate ways to let out steam or frustration, like banging on pots or squeezing a soft toy, as well as acknowledging and validating their feelings, are all essential strategies for assisting them in expressing and managing their emotions.

What should I do in social circumstances if my infant exhibits shyness or hesitation?

It is best to respect your baby's comfort level and refrain from pressuring them to interact before they are ready if they appear bashful or hesitant in social circumstances. Encourage and support them gently, and allow them to acclimate to new social situations at their rate.

How can I encourage compassion and empathy in my baby's social interactions?

Empathy and kindness can be fostered by praising your child for acts of kindness or empathy toward others, pointing out and categorizing emotions in others during social interactions, and modeling compassionate and caring behavior yourself.

How can I foster my infant's curiosity and desire to explore unfamiliar social settings?

By introducing your infant to a range of social environments, including playgroups, family get-togethers, and neighborhood activities, and by offering them gentle assistance and encouragement as they navigate new situations, you may foster their curiosity and interest.

What are some strategies for helping my baby develop relationships that are based on security and trust?
To help your baby feel secure and trusted, you should attend to their needs regularly, be sensitive to their requirements, soothe and reassure them when they are in distress, and keep regular routines and rituals that help them feel stable.

How can I foster an awareness of other people's feelings and empathy in my child?
By exhibiting empathy yourself, identifying and categorizing others' feelings in social situations, and giving your child opportunities to see and participate in acts of kindness toward others, you may support your infant's development of empathy.

What should I do if my child exhibits possessiveness or jealousy toward other caregivers or siblings?
When your infant exhibits jealousy or possessiveness, provide them opportunities to bond positively and supportively with

other caregivers or siblings, acknowledge their feelings without passing judgment, and reassure them of your love and attention.

How can I encourage my infant's growing feeling of self-sufficiency and independence?

Allowing your baby to explore and learn about their surroundings at their own pace, providing options within safe bounds, and promoting self-help abilities like feeding themselves or getting dressed with aid are all essential ways to support their sense of independence.

What are some methods for assisting my child in becoming a good communicator?

Reacting quickly to your baby's attempts at communication, supporting vocal communication with basic gestures and signs, and creating a rich language environment with lots of opportunities for speaking and listening are all strategies for helping your baby develop communication skills.

How can I support my child in resolving disputes or conflicts with siblings or peers?

By teaching them primary language or gestures to communicate their emotions, modeling constructive conflict resolution techniques, and closely monitoring interactions to guarantee everyone's safety and well-being, you may assist your infant in resolving problems.

What are some telltale signs that my child is developing healthy bonds with siblings or peers?

Playing together with others, sharing toys and taking turns, demonstrating empathy and caring for the well-being of others, and actively seeking out social contacts with known people are all indications of healthy relationships.

How can I encourage my infant's social and emotional development to be resilient and adaptable?

Encouraging problem-solving and coping techniques, creating a loving and supportive atmosphere, and assisting your child in gaining self-efficacy and confidence in their capacity to overcome obstacles are all part of fostering resilience.

What part does providing responsive care play in my infant's social and emotional development?

Healthy social and emotional development is facilitated by responsive caring, which entails observing your baby's cues and signals, responding to their needs promptly and sensitively, and building a safe and loving bond.

Language and communication phases that babies go through

How might I support my infant's language development in regular conversations?

Talking to your baby throughout the day, naming things and describing what you are doing, reacting to their vocalizations and babbling, and routinely reading to them are all ways to promote language development.

What indicators indicate my infant is starting to pick up words and basic commands?

When your baby responds to their name, follows simple instructions like "wave bye-bye," and looks at familiar things when mentioned, these are indications that they are starting to understand words and simple orders.

When can I anticipate hearing my child pronounce their first words?

While the exact timing varies, most newborns speak for the first time between 9 and 12 months. Continue conversing with your infant and support their communication attempts.

What are some strategies for fostering my child's developing linguistic abilities?

Please encourage your child to learn new words and concepts, engage in back-and-forth discussions, mimic their sounds and movements, and reinforce verbal communication with gestures or sign language.

How can I support my baby's development of babbling patterns and early spoken sounds?

Playing simple games like "peekaboo," singing nursery rhymes with repetitive sounds, and making exaggerated facial expressions to encourage imitation are all effective ways to support your baby's development of early speech sounds and babbling patterns.

Should I be worried if my child is not babbling or making noises at this age?

Although most babies start babbling between six and nine months, the exact moment varies. Talk to your pediatrician about your concerns about whether your baby isn't babbling or producing noises by the time they are ten months old to rule out any underlying problems.

How can I increase the vocabulary and linguistic comprehension of my infant?

By utilizing descriptive language, introducing new words and concepts during routine activities, and giving your infant a chance to engage with various people and objects, you may help them develop their vocabulary and language comprehension.

What are some strategies to support my child's reading and book interests?

Incorporate regular story-time rituals, select age-appropriate board books with vibrant illustrations and straightforward language, and let your child explore and handle books independently to spark their interest in reading and books.

How can I help my infant learn to point and gesture as a means of nonverbal communication?

By utilizing gestures and facial expressions, reacting quickly and positively to your baby's attempts to point or gesture, and creating opportunities for shared experiences and joint attention, you may help your baby develop nonverbal communication abilities.

How does responsive communication affect the language development of my infant?

A solid foundation for language development is created by responsive communication, which is listening to and reacting to your baby's attempts at communication. It also motivates your baby to keep experimenting and exploring with language.

How can I help my infant develop communication skills through sign language?

Sign language can be incorporated by teaching basic signs for ordinary words like "more," "eat," and "all done" and then modeling the signals while pronouncing the associated word.

What are some strategies for getting my infant to communicate with others conversationally?

Encourage your baby to engage in conversation by pausing during exchanges, waiting for their response, taking turns babbling or making noises, and giving them lots of praise when they attempt to communicate.

Should I be worried if my infant isn't making distinct consonant sounds by this age?

Though the exact timing varies, most babies start experimenting with consonant sounds like "m," "b," and "d" between the ages of 7 and 10 months. See your pediatrician or a speech-language pathologist if you have concerns about your child's speech development.

How can I use language to help my infant grasp cause and effect?

Use primary language to explain actions and consequences to your baby during daily activities. For example, "When you push the button, the music plays" or "If you drop the toy, it falls." It will help your baby comprehend cause and effect.

What part does singing play in the linguistic development of my baby?

Exposing your infant to rhythm, melody, and language patterns through singing can promote language development and improve their ability to comprehend auditory information. To keep your baby interested, sing nursery rhymes and well-known songs frequently.

How can I help my kid communicate through body language and gestures?

By mimicking your baby's movements, responding favorably to their attempts at communication, and giving them opportunities to express themselves nonverbally throughout play and interactions, you may encourage your baby to use gestures and body language.

What are some indicators that my infant is starting to pick up on more intricate linguistic ideas?

When your infant follows multistep instructions, answers questions correctly, and expresses interest in discussions around them, they start to grasp more sophisticated language concepts.

How can I provide my infant with a language-rich environment?

You may create a language-rich environment by talking to your baby often throughout the day, narrating your activities and the things around them, and exposing them to various interactive toys, books, and songs that encourage language development.

Should I correct my baby when they mispronounce words or make verbal errors?

It is not the time to correct your baby's mispronunciations or speech problems; they are still learning and exploring language. Instead, promote their communication attempts and provide an example of proper pronunciation.

How can I help my infant develop their language comprehension and expand vocabulary?

Provide opportunities for your baby to explore and engage with their surroundings, name things and actions throughout daily activities, and introduce new words in context to support their developing vocabulary and language comprehension.

The emotional growth and attachment of newborns

During this period, how does my infant build a bond with caregivers?

When caregivers are responsive and consistent—that is, they attend to the baby's needs in a timely and considerate manner attachment develops. Your newborn may exhibit attachment behaviors by clinging to known caregivers for solace, exhibiting distress when taken from them, and expressing happiness when reuniting.

What are some telltale indicators that my child is developing strong bonds?

When a caregiver is present, a child in a secure attachment will confidently explore their surroundings, seek comfort from them when they are upset, and exhibit signs of distress when separated but immediately settle down when reunited.

How can I strengthen my relationship with my infant during this phase?

By using responsive and caring parenting techniques, such as holding, snuggling, and comforting your baby when required, reacting quickly to their cues and signals, and creating a secure and encouraging atmosphere, you can strengthen your relationship with your baby.

What part does my baby's emotional development play in responsive parenting?

The basis for a baby's healthy emotional development and attachment is laid by responsive parenting, which is when caregivers regularly respond to the baby's needs with warmth and sensitivity. It builds emotional stability and trust in the caregiver-infant relationship.

How can I be a secure attachment parent and still encourage my baby's developing feelings of independence?

Encourage a balance between independence and connection in your baby by giving them opportunities for self-expression and exploration in a secure and comforting setting, all while supporting their developing sense of autonomy.

What are some strategies for helping my baby develop emotional control?

Encourage emotional control in your child by being there for them in times of need, offering consolation and assurance, modeling peaceful and constructive coping mechanisms like deep breathing or soft rocking, and establishing a reliable routine that makes your child feel safe.

What should I do if my infant exhibits signs of anxiety or reluctance when they are among strangers?

If your infant exhibits signs of anxiety or hesitancy around strange people or circumstances, comfort and reassure them while introducing them to new experiences gradually in a helpful way. It will give them time to get used to the new environment and feel safe.

How can I help my infant develop empathy and comprehension of the feelings of others?

Encourage the development of empathy in your child by showing kindness and compassion in your relationships with others, recognizing and validating your baby's feelings, creating chances for social engagement, and paying attention to the emotions and reactions of others.

What are some indicators my child is starting to recognize and react to other people's feelings?

Your baby may mimic facial expressions or movements, exhibit empathy or worry when someone else is distressed, or seek comfort from caregivers when they witness others in distress as indicators that they are starting to understand and react to emotions in others.

If I am worried about my baby's emotional growth or attachment, when should I get help?

Seek support if you have concerns about your baby's emotional development or attachment, such as chronic problems in developing stable attachments, intense anguish upon separation, or worrying behavioral or emotional responses that interfere with everyday functioning.

If I work outside the home, what are some methods to help my infant develop a healthy attachment relationship?

Foster a stable attachment bond by maximizing quality time with your infant when you're together, engaging in responsive and interactive caregiving practices, and keeping consistent routines and rituals to provide comfort and predictability.

How can I assist my baby's emotional development as they encounter new feelings such as frustration or disappointment?

Support your baby's emotional development by acknowledging and validating their feelings, offering comfort and reassurance during distress, and modeling appropriate coping methods such as deep breathing or switching focus to a comforting activity.

What should I do if my kid displays signs of separation anxiety during this stage?

If your infant shows signs of separation anxiety, such as clinging to caregivers or protesting when separated, reassure them of your presence and availability, set consistent goodbye routines, and progressively expose them to short separations to help build trust and security.

How can I foster my baby's social development and peer relationships at this age?

Encourage social development and peer interactions by arranging playdates with other infants or joining parent-child programs or organizations where your baby can connect with peers in a friendly and monitored atmosphere.

What are some methods to increase my baby's emotional resilience and coping abilities?

Promote emotional resilience and coping abilities by providing opportunities for your infant to encounter and overcome minor problems or frustrations, offering comfort and support when required, and modeling positive coping strategies in your behavior.

How can I encourage my baby's emotional expression and communication?

Support emotional expression and communication by acknowledging and responding to your baby's facial expressions, gestures, and vocalizations and allowing them to express their emotions through play, art, or music.

What part does connection play in my baby's sense of security and exploration?

Attachment provides a solid basis from which your infant can explore their world and engage with others, knowing that caregivers are available for support and comfort when required, which fosters confidence and independence in exploration.

Should I be concerned if my baby seems more reserved or cautious in social situations?

Babies develop social skills at their own rate, and some may be more reserved or cautious in social situations than others. Respect your baby's temperament and provide support and encouragement as they navigate social interactions and new experiences.

How can I encourage my baby's emotional development when they demand independence?

Support your baby's emotional development by allowing options and opportunities for independent exploration and decision-making within safe bounds while providing guidance, comfort, and support as they navigate new challenges and experiences.

When should I seek professional guidance if I have concerns about my baby's emotional development or attachment?

Seek professional help if you have concerns about your baby's emotional development or attachment, such as chronic problems in building stable bonds, intense emotional discomfort, or worrying behavioral patterns that interfere with everyday functioning or relationships.

Chapter Four

Feeding and nutrition development in kids

How do babies between the ages of 7 and 10 months acquire their eating and nutrition skills?

As infants transition from being solely breastfed or formula-fed to exploring a variety of solid foods and experimenting with different flavors and textures, their feeding and nutritional development progresses.

What signals indicate that my child is prepared to begin eating solid food?

When your baby can sit up with assistance, show curiosity in other people's meals, and transfer food from the front of their mouth to the rear and swallow it, they are ready for solid foods.

Which meals are suitable for my kid as a first at this age?

Iron-fortified newborn cereals combined with breast milk or formula and single-ingredient purees of fruits and vegetables like mashed bananas, sweet potatoes, or avocados are appropriate first foods to introduce.

How can I get my infant to sample different foods and flavors?

By providing a range of tastes and textures, letting your baby feed themselves with age-appropriate finger foods, and setting an example of healthy eating habits by indulging in a range of wholesome meals, you can encourage your baby to explore new foods and flavors.

At this age, what part of my baby's diet does nursing or formula feeding still play?

After your baby consumes solid foods, breastfeeding or formula feeding will continue to give them the vital nutrition, water, and immune support they need. Until the child is at least 12 months old, the primary source of sustenance should continue to be breast milk or formula.

How can I make sure my child's food contains adequate iron?

You can ensure your kid gets enough iron by providing iron-rich foods such as fortified cereals, pureed meats, poultry, fish, beans, and lentils. Talk to your pediatrician about any worries about how much iron you consume.

What typical feeding difficulties can parents have at this point?

Common feeding issues include refusals to eat during meals, intolerance to new foods or textures, and trouble making the switch to solid foods. These difficulties are frequently transient and can be overcome with perseverance and patience.

How can I keep my infant from choking when introducing solid foods?

By providing suitable foods cut into tiny, manageable pieces, avoiding hard foods, small, spherical, or sticky foods, watching your infant during meals, and encouraging them to chew thoroughly, you can reduce the risk of choking risks.

What part does responsive feeding play in my baby's nutrition and feeding development?

Healthy eating habits and preferences are shaped by responsive feeding, which includes identifying and attending to your baby's signals of hunger and fullness, encouraging self-control, and providing a range of nutrient-dense meals in a comforting setting.

How can I ease the transition to drinking from a cup or sippy cup, and when should I offer it?

Around six to nine months of age, you can start introducing drinking from a cup or sippy cup. Offer modest quantities of water, formula, or breast milk in an open cup or a transitional sippy cup with handles. Make the gradual switch from bottle to cup.

How can I ensure my infant gets adequate nutrition from only solid food?

You can ensure they are getting enough nutrients by providing your infant with a range of nutrient-dense foods, including fruits, vegetables, grains, foods high in protein, and dairy products. A balanced diet should contain items from every food category.

What are the telltale indicators of a food allergy or intolerance in my baby?

Rash, hives, swelling, vomiting, diarrhea, or trouble breathing soon after eating a particular food are symptoms of a food allergy or intolerance. See your pediatrician for additional testing if you think your child may have a food allergy or intolerance.

How can I properly introduce my infant to foods that cause allergies, such as eggs, peanuts, and seafood?

One by one, introduce allergenic foods to your infant in little doses while keeping an eye out for any suggestions of an allergic reaction. To help lower the chance of food allergies, incorporate these items into your diet regularly and at an early age.

What are some tactics for handling conflicts over meals or fussy eating habits?

Some strategies for handling mealtime conflicts are offering a range of foods in little, controllable portions, letting your baby explore and engage with their food, and keeping a calm and cheerful mealtime atmosphere.

How can I help my baby switch to family dinners and table foods?

By giving your baby a range of foods from your plate, letting them feed themselves with the proper utensils, and including them in family mealtime rituals and conversations, you can help your baby transition to table foods and family meals.

If my infant rejects particular foods or textures, what should I do?

Offer meals or textures your baby rejects again later, maybe prepared differently or combined with comfort foods they like. Remain persistent and patient, and refrain from forcing food on your infant.

How can I make sure my infant drinks enough water during the day?

Offer your baby water, breast milk, or formula in between meals and snacks to ensure they keep hydrated. Juice and other sugary drinks should not be served since they are high in empty calories and might cause tooth decay.

What are some indicators my child might be prepared to stop receiving formula or breast milk?

Your baby may be ready to wean when they show less interest in nursing or using a bottle, consume a more comprehensive range of solid foods, and can use a cup or sippy cup independently.

What part does responsive feeding play in keeping people from being overfed or underfed?

Allowing your infant to self-regulate their food intake based on hunger and fullness cues helps minimize overfeeding and underfeeding. When your baby shows signs of being full, stop feeding them. Offer food when they are hungry.

How can I securely introduce finger foods, and when should I do so?

You can start introducing finger foods around seven or eight months of age. Start with soft, easily-grasp items like cooked fruits and vegetables and little pieces of well-cooked pasta or bread. When your baby is eating, keep a watchful eye on them and don't give them anything that could choke them.

Chapter Five

How babies develop in terms of sleep and rest:

How do babies between the ages of 7 and 10 months acquire their ability to sleep and rest?

This stage of sleep and rest development is characterized by longer stretches of sleep at night, more regular nap times, and greater freedom in falling asleep and taking care of oneself.

What sleep schedules do babies seven to ten months old usually follow?

At this age, babies typically sleep for 11 to 12 hours per night, with fewer and fewer awakenings during the night. In addition, they might take two or three naps during the day for two to three hours of sleep.

How do I get my infant to follow a regular sleep schedule at this age?

A regular bedtime and nap schedule, a relaxing nighttime ritual like taking a bath, reading, and cuddling, and creating a sleep-friendly atmosphere with cozy bedding and dim lighting are all essential components of a consistent sleep schedule.

What kinds of typical sleep issues can parents face at this point?

Nighttime awakenings, trouble falling back asleep following feedings or other sleep disruptions, and aversion to naps or bedtime are common sleep issues. These difficulties are frequently transient and are solvable with persistence and patience.

How can I help my baby learn to comfort themselves and go to sleep on their own?

Provide comfort objects like a stuffed animal or favorite blanket, put your baby to bed sleepy but awake, and offer comfort and reassurance without taking them up immediately if they wake up throughout the night to promote self-soothing and independent sleep.

What impact does napping throughout the day have on sleep quality at night?

Maintaining a regular nap schedule daily aids in your baby's sleep-wake cycle regulation. It can enhance the quality of their nocturnal sleep by lowering excessive fatigue and encouraging more profound, more restorative sleep.

When my baby gets closer to their first birthday, how can I help them adjust to taking fewer naps?

By gradually increasing waking times between naps, combining naps into more extended sleep periods, and modifying nap timings to correspond with your baby's natural sleep cycles, you can facilitate your baby's transition to fewer naps.

What should I do if my kid wakes up or disturbs me often at night?

Try to determine and treat any possible reasons your baby may wake up during the night, such as hunger, pain, or teething. It might also be beneficial to have a regular bedtime routine and to calmly and regularly attend to your baby's needs.

How can I make my baby's environment conducive to sleep?

Establish a peaceful, dark, and quiet sleeping area for your infant; keep the room's temperature reasonable; and use white noise or calming music to block out distracting sounds.

Which indications indicate a baby being prepared to move from a crib to a toddler bed?

Exhibiting an interest in transitioning to a giant bed, climbing out of the crib, or outgrowing the crib's dimensions indicates that your child might be ready for a toddler bed. You may want to consider switching to a toddler bed after your kid is between 18 and 24 months old and can comprehend safety instructions.

How can I assist my infant in acclimating to a regular sleep schedule?

By awakening your child at the same time every morning, establishing regular nap periods, and upholding a normal bedtime routine, you may help them develop a consistent sleep schedule.

If my infant has nightmares or night terrors, should I be concerned?

While nightmares and night terrors are frequent in babies, they usually go away independently. If your baby is upset, comfort them; try not to wake them up entirely since this could prolong the event.

What can I do if my infant wakes up early and won't go back to sleep?

Try consoling and reassuring your baby if they wake up early, but also encourage them to remain in their crib until it's time for them to wake up. Steer clear of bright lighting and stimulating activities that could exacerbate their sleep disturbances.

Can I put my kid to sleep with a lovey or pacifier?

Sleeping with a pacifier or little lovey is usually fine after a baby can roll over and move objects away from their face. But, keep an eye on your child as they sleep and make sure these things are age- and safety-appropriate.

How can I determine whether my infant is sleeping well overall?

Having a regular sleep schedule without excessive daytime tiredness or nightly awakenings, completing developmental milestones, and being attentive and content during wakeful hours all indicate you are getting enough sleep.

What should I do if my baby's sleep patterns are disturbed due to travel or schedule changes?

When traveling or experiencing routine shifts, keep your baby's sleep schedule as consistent as possible. Returning home should be done with familiar things from home, familiar nighttime routines, and time to get used to the new routine.

How can I help my infant sleep through the night for more prolonged periods?

You may encourage longer durations of nocturnal sleep by ensuring your baby is fed and comfortable before bed, developing a soothing bedtime routine, and setting up a sleep environment promoting restful sleep.

Should I be concerned if my infant is still awake for night feedings at this age?

At this age, it's common for newborns to still wake up for nightly feedings, mainly if they're breastfed. When your baby wakes up in the middle of the night, calm and reassure them, but if you are worried about their feeding patterns, speak with your pediatrician first.

How does sleeping during the day affect my baby's general sleep patterns?

Napping during the day is essential for your baby's general sleep patterns since it gives them a chance to recuperate and consolidate everything they've learned and experienced during the day. Maintain a regular nap schedule to encourage restful sleep at night.

When should I get my baby's sleep problems checked out by a pediatric sleep specialist?

If you are worried about your baby's overall sleep duration and quality, or if your baby's sleep problems aren't improving despite your best attempts to treat them, consider consulting a pediatric sleep specialist.

Infants' developments relating to phases of sleep patterns and routines

How many naps should my kid take at this age, and how long?

Most newborns at this age will generally take two naps daily, lasting around 1 to 2 hours. However, individual sleep demands might differ, so study your baby's indications and alter their nap schedule accordingly.

Is it common for my baby's sleep patterns to shift at this age?

Yes, it's usual for newborns' sleep patterns to alter as they grow and develop. Your infant may experience changes in nap length, frequency, or nightly sleep habits, which can be influenced by growth spurts, teething, or developmental milestones.

How can I build a consistent sleep routine for my baby?

Create a reliable bedtime routine by locating a peaceful and predictable series of activities leading up to bedtime, such as washing, reading a book, and singing a lullaby. Keep the routine regular each night to tell your infant it's time for sleep.

What should I do if my baby's sleep becomes disrupted due to teething or developmental milestones?

If your baby's sleep is disrupted due to teething or developmental milestones, offer comfort and soothing tactics such as gently rocking or hugging. Provide a quiet and consistent bedtime ritual to help your infant feel secure and relaxed before sleep.

What strategies can be employed to promote self-soothing and facilitate a resumption of sleep in children who experience nocturnal awakenings?

Encourage self-soothing by providing your baby opportunities to experience falling asleep independently, such as placing them in their cot while drowsy but still awake. Offer comfort and reassurance if needed, but gradually help your baby learn to calm themselves back to sleep.

Should I be concerned if my baby is not sleeping through the night by this age?

Every baby is different, and some may still require overnight feedings or wakeups at this age. However, if your infant routinely has difficulties sleeping through the night or suffers frequent night waking that affects their sleep and yours, speak with your pediatrician for help.

What can I do if my baby's sleep regression goes beyond a few weeks?

If your baby's sleep regression persists beyond a few weeks or significantly disrupts their sleep quality and daytime functioning, try evaluating your baby's sleep environment, routine, and calming practices. Consult with a pediatric sleep specialist if needed for additional help and direction.

How can I assist my baby in adjusting to transitions in their sleep habit, such as moving to a new sleep environment or switching to one nap a day?

Help your baby adjust to alterations in their sleep schedule by gradually introducing changes, such as gradually transitioning to a new sleep location or modifying nap durations by modest increments. Provide warmth and constancy during the transition to help your infant feel secure.

What impact do daytime routine and activity level play in my baby's nocturnal sleep patterns?

A steady daily schedule and appropriate physical activity might assist in regulating your baby's sleep-wake cycle and encourage improved nighttime sleep. Ensure your kid has lots of daytime playing and outdoor time to expend energy and maintain a consistent daily regimen.

When should I explore sleep training approaches for my baby?

Consider sleep training approaches if your baby has difficulty falling asleep or staying asleep independently and if their sleep patterns significantly impact your family's well-being and functioning. Getting guidance from a pediatrician or a sleep specialist regarding sleep training tactics suitable for the child's age is advisable.

What can I do if my infant develops separation anxiety at bedtime?

If your baby develops separation anxiety at bedtime, soothe them with a pleasant bedtime routine and provide a transitional object, For instance, a cherished plush toy or covering, to provide them with a sense of safety. Gradually increase the space between you and your baby during sleep procedures to develop independence.

Is it common for my kids to wake up at night and cry even if they previously slept through the night?

Yes, babies are normal to wake up in the middle of the night and cry, especially when they're teething, reaching developmental milestones, or sick. While consoling and reassuring your infant can help them fall back asleep, try not to overstimulate or satisfy them if they wake up at night.

How can I make my baby's sleeping surroundings more comfortable?

Ensure your baby's room is quiet, dark, and appropriately calm to create a suitable sleep environment. Use white noise or gentle music to block background noise and potential sleep disruptors like bright lights or technological devices.

What should I do if travel or other changes in habit cause my baby's sleep schedule to be disturbed?

Try to persist as dependably as possible with bedtime and naptime routines if your baby's sleep schedule is disturbed by travel or other disruptions. By progressively moving bedtime and nap times closer to the intended timetable, you can gradually become used to the new routine.

How can I teach my infant to sleep independently without using sleep aids like nursing or rocking?

Reduce your dependency on sleep aids like rocking or nursing to promote independent sleep. Establish a regular bedtime routine and progressively remove yourself from your baby's sleep environment so they can learn to comfort themselves and sleep independently.

What are some indicators that my child is prepared to go from taking multiple naps during the day?

When your baby regularly refuses to take the morning nap, naps longer in the afternoon, and sticks to a regular bedtime routine even with only one nap per day, it's time to move them to a single nap.

How can I help my infant develop sound sleeping patterns that will carry over into toddlerhood?

You can cultivate healthy sleep habits by implementing a consistent sleep routine, creating a calming twilight practice, and encouraging autonomous sleep abilities. Promote long-term sleep independence, assist self-soothing, and create a comfortable sleeping environment.

What effect does food have on my baby's routine and sleep patterns?

Your baby's eating habits might affect their sleep cycles and routines, mainly if they are ravenous or stuffed before bed. To encourage sound sleep, ensure your infant eats a healthy diet and provide a balanced supper or snack before bed.

How can I nurse my kid at night without upsetting their sleep schedule?

Reduce stimulation and have brief interactions with your infant when handling night feedings. Feed your baby in a calm, dark area; do not play or do anything stimulating that can keep them from falling back asleep.

If my efforts don't resolve my baby's sleep problems, when should I get expert assistance?

See your physician or a sleep specialist for additional assessment and advice if your infant continues to struggle with sleep problems despite your best attempts to help them develop healthy sleep patterns or if their sleep disturbances substantially influence their development or well-being.

Chapter Six

The health and treatment stages of infants

My infant seems to be growing more curious and active. How can I make sure they're safe while they investigate their environment?

Babyproofing your home is crucial as your child grows more mobile. It involves putting safety gates in place, covering outlets, fastening furniture, and keeping small things out of reach. When your baby is playing, keep a watchful eye on them and provide safe items for them to explore.

How can I help my child practice proper dental hygiene?

When your baby's teeth erupt, you may promote good oral hygiene by cleaning them with a soft-bristled toothbrush and fluoride-free toothpaste and gently wiping their gums with a spotless, wet cloth after feedings. A bottle should not be used to put your infant to sleep since this can lead to tooth rot.

A rash has appeared on my baby's skin. How do I handle this, and what might be the cause?

Numerous things, such as drooling, eczema, heat, or irritant contact, can result in rashes. Avoid using strong soaps or detergents on the afflicted regions, and instead, use a mild moisturizer or diaper rash ointment without any smell. Speak with your pediatrician if the rash doesn't go away or gets worse.

Which foods should I offer my infant initially, and what are some indicators that they might be ready to move to table foods?

Your baby may be ready for table foods if they can sit up without assistance, show interest in what you are eating, and demonstrate that they can chew or mash food with their gums. Table meals such as cooked fruits, vegetables, soft meats, smooth, mashed, or pureed foods can be introduced.

Constipation is starting to set in for my infant. How can I assist in easing their pain?

Give your kid lots of fluids to assist in easing constipation; if they are older than six months, this can include breast milk, formula, or water. Add high-fiber items to their diet, such as puréed pears, prunes, or peas, and gently massage their abdomen to encourage loose stools.

Is my infant's separation anxiety typical for this age group?

Yes, as babies become more aware of their environment and form bonds with caregivers, separation anxiety is frequent. Offer comfort items like a preferred toy or blanket, create a predictable schedule, and reassure your infant with calming words and gestures.

How can I ease my baby's discomfort during teething?

Offering your infant icy teething rings or toys to chew on, gently massaging their gums with clean fingertips, and offering comfort and assurance during this challenging period will all help reduce teething discomfort. Your pediatrician might suggest over-the-counter painkillers.

When does my baby's fever need to be treated, and what should I do if it does?

To avoid dehydration, keep a constant eye on your baby's temperature and provide drinks if they start to fever. If your infant is older than three months or younger than three months, and if an individual experiences a rectal temperature of 100.4°F (38°C) or higher, it is advisable to contact their pediatrician.

My infant is starting to fight to go to bed and has difficulty staying asleep. How can I support the development of sound sleeping practices?

Create a peaceful and restful sleeping environment, stick to a regular bedtime schedule, and provide consolation and assurance when you wake up in the middle of the night. When it's almost time for bed, steer clear of stimulating activities and help your infant learn how to comfort themselves if they wake up throughout the night.

Should I be worried if my child is not reaching developmental milestones at this age?

Even though every baby develops differently, monitoring your child's development and talking to your pediatrician about any worries is essential. Early intervention can frequently address developmental delays, guaranteeing your youngster gets the required help.

My baby has begun to cough and have congestion in his nasal passages. How may I assist in easing their discomfort?

By using a bulb syringe to gently suction mucus from your baby's nose, using a saline nasal spray or drops to loosen phlegm, and keeping the air moist in their room with a cool mist humidifier, you can assist in relieving nasal congestion. See your pediatrician if your baby's symptoms worsen or stay the same.

What are some indicators of infant dehydration, and how may it be avoided?

Dehydrated infants may exhibit sunken fontanelles (soft areas on the head), dark yellow urine, dry lips, and reduced frequency of wet diaper changes. Mainly during high temperatures or when your infant is unwell, offer breast milk, formula, or water frequently to prevent dehydration. You should also monitor your baby's urine output and general state of hydration.

My baby's eczema has begun to manifest. What are some strategies for treating their ailments?

Keeping your baby's skin well-hydrated with a mild, fragrance-free moisturizer or emollient, avoiding the use of harsh soaps or detergents, dressing them in soft, breathable clothing, and using a humidifier to give moisture to their surroundings are all important ways to treat the symptoms of eczema. See your pediatrician for additional assessment and treatment if your child's eczema worsens or persists.

My baby fell or sustained a minor injury. How can I tell if I need to see a doctor?

Minor wounds, such as bumps, bruises, or cuts, can frequently be treated at home using simple first aid techniques, including washing the area with warm soapy water and bandaging it. Seek prompt medical assistance, nevertheless, if your baby sustains a head injury, loses consciousness, or exhibits any other symptoms of a more severe injury.

If my infant inadvertently consumes anything possibly hazardous, what should I do?

Should your infant swallow something that could be dangerous, including medicine, household cleaner, or toxic plant, get in touch with poison control or your neighborhood emergency services right away. Until doctors tell you to, avoid making your baby throw up and attempt to figure out what your infant swallowed.

How can I aid in my child's recovery from a respiratory illness or cold?

By ensuring your baby gets enough sleep, providing drinks to prevent dehydration, using a cool mist humidifier to relieve congestion, and carefully suctioning mucus from their nose using a bulb syringe or nasal aspirator, you can aid in their recovery from a cold or respiratory illness. See your pediatrician if your child's symptoms worsen or don't go away.

My infant has a diaper rash doesn't seem to go better with simple fixes. How should I proceed?

See your pediatrician if applying diaper rash cream and keeping the affected region dry and clean don't help your baby's diaper rash. They might suggest an alternative course of action or assess whether the rash is caused by an underlying illness such as a yeast infection.

What are some strategies to help my infant healthily develop teeth?

After feedings, wipe your baby's gums with a clean, damp towel to encourage good dental development. Once teeth sprout, start cleaning their teeth with a soft-bristled toothbrush and fluoride-free toothpaste. To prevent tooth decay, limit sugary meals and beverages and refrain from giving your kid a bottle before bed.

My baby's digestive problems, including gas or bloating, have started. How can I assist in easing their pain?

By making sure your baby is burped often during feedings, gently massaging their abdomen in a clockwise direction, and providing tummy time to help release trapped gas, you can help relieve digestive concerns like gas or bloating. If you continue to have stomach problems, see your pediatrician for additional testing and advice.

How can I make sure my child gets suitable medical attention and shots at this developmental stage?

See your pediatrician for routine well-baby checks to track your child's growth and development and to obtain the needed immunizations. Keep yourself updated on your child's immunization schedule, and talk to your pediatrician about any worries or inquiries you may have.

The teething and comfort stages that babies go through

What are some telltale indicators of my baby's teething?

Increased drooling, swollen or sensitive gums, fussiness or irritability, biting on objects, and irregular sleep indicate your infant is teething. Some babies may also experience mild diarrhea or a slight temperature during teething.

How can I ease my infant's suffering while they are teething?

By giving your infant cold teething rings or safe teething toys to gnaw on, you can help ease their discomfort during teething. Relief can be obtained by gently massaging the gums with a clean finger or a cold, watery towel. Additionally, a pediatrician's supervision may utilize over-the-counter teething gels or pain medications.

When teething, is it cause for concern if my kid exhibits moderate signs like drooling and fussiness?

During teething, mild symptoms like drooling and fussiness are typical and typically don't need medical attention. But keep an eye out for any indications of more severe pain or issues, including a high fever or an inability to feed, and speak with your physician if you have any worries.

How can I calm my infant down if they are in pain from ear aches associated with teething?

Provide your infant with comfort and gentle reassurance to ease their earache caused by teething. Under a pediatrician's supervision, you can also attempt putting a warm compress on the afflicted ear or using over-the-counter painkillers like acetaminophen or ibuprofen.

Is it possible for teething to interfere with my baby's sleep schedule?

Indeed, teething can interfere with your baby's sleep schedule because it makes them uncomfortable and irritable. To facilitate your infant's resumption of sleep, employ soothing and tranquil techniques. If your infant is experiencing pain, it may be advisable to contemplate administering pain management.

What are some natural ways to soothe my infant who is teething?

Non-pharmaceutical ways to soothe a teething infant include giving them icy teething toys or cool washcloths to gnaw on, using a clean finger to gently massage their gums, giving them additional cuddles and calming activities, and sticking to a regular bedtime schedule to encourage sound sleep.

Should I stop nursing or bottle-feeding my baby if they are having trouble teething?

Even though teething discomfort might cause some babies to reject nursing or bottle-feed temporarily, it's crucial to keep providing breast milk or formula to ensure that kids get enough nutrients and fluids. To help ease discomfort, you can give a cold teething toy or comfort before eating.

What part does sucking or comfort breastfeeding play in calming a teething infant?

A teething baby may find some momentary relief from their discomfort by comfort feeding or sucking, which offers solace and diversion. Let your baby nurse or suckle as needed, but keep an eye out for indications that they rely too much on this comfort feeding method.

Can my infant get diaper rash or other skin irritations from teething?

Drooling associated with teething can make the area surrounding your baby's lips and chin more wet, which could cause diaper rash or skin irritation. Keep the afflicted regions clean and dry to avoid irritation, apply petroleum jelly or barrier cream as needed, and change wet or soiled diapers very away.

When do I need to contact a doctor if my infant seems to be having severe or ongoing teething symptoms?

If your infant is having severe or chronic teething symptoms, such as a high temperature, heavy drooling, reluctance to eat or drink, or signs of dehydration—seek medical attention. In addition, if you are worried about your baby's general health or wellness, contact your pediatrician.

How can I ease my teething baby's suffering at night?

Provide a soothing bedtime routine for your teething baby, such as soft rocking or hugging, before putting them in their crib to help them cope with night's discomfort. Give them a cool, clean teething toy or washcloth to gnaw on if they wake up in pain.

When teething, is there a cause for concern if my infant drools excessively?

During teething, excessive drooling is normal and typically not a reason for concern. Keep your baby's neck and chin clean and dry to avoid skin irritation or rash. See your pediatrician if the excessive drooling continues or if other symptoms accompany it.

Can my baby's appetite or eating habits alter as they are teething?

Due to discomfort or irritation around the gums, teething may momentarily alter your baby's appetite or feeding habits. Provide excellent or soft meals that are easy on their gums, including yogurt or chilled fruit purees. Also, ensure they drink enough water, breast milk, or formula to be hydrated.

How can I ease the discomfort my teething infant feels at mealtimes?

Offer your teething infant soft or cooled foods that are gentle on their gums to help them manage their discomfort during mealtimes. Steer clear of crunchy or firm meals that could aggravate gum inflammation, and give your child lots of reassurance and consoling hugs while they're nursing.

Is it typical for my baby to become irritable or experience mood swings when teething?

Yes, because of their discomfort and irregular sleep habits during teething, babies usually experience mood swings or irritability. Offer reassurance and calming methods like singing, hugging, or light massages to ease their discomfort.

Can my infant get diaper rash or diarrhea from teething?

While increased drooling during teething may result in loose stools or diaper rash due to skin sensitivity, teething alone usually does not cause diarrhea. To prevent diaper rash, use petroleum jelly or barrier cream to keep the diaper region clean and dry.

What are some natural solutions I might use to ease the pain my teething baby is experiencing?

Chilled teething toys or washcloths, frozen banana or breast milk popsicles, and herbal therapies like chamomile tea (when used cautiously and under the advice of a healthcare provider) are some natural remedies to relieve the discomfort associated with teething. When giving your infant any teething medication, always keep an eye on them.

Is it cause for concern if my infant has trouble falling asleep or wakes up a lot at night because of teething discomfort?

While your baby's teething discomfort may momentarily disturb their sleep schedule, ongoing trouble falling asleep or frequent nighttime awakenings may point to more severe problems. See your baby's pediatrician if their sleep issues continue or have a substantial adverse influence on their health.

How can I make my teething baby more at ease when changing diapers?

Minimize disturbance to your teething infant during diaper changes by changing their diaper quickly and efficiently.

Throughout the diaper change, provide a distraction (such as a favorite toy or soft music) and comforting words of support.

What are some indicators that my baby's teething pain might be more severe and need medical help?

If your infant is having severe or ongoing diarrhea, won't eat or drink, cries or fusses a lot, or shows signs of dehydration, then their teething discomfort may be more severe and need medical treatment. Contact your pediatrician if you are worried about your baby's health or well-being.

About the Author

ADEGBOYE S. ADURAGBEMI is an African manager, business administrator, entrepreneur, and motivational speaker. ADEGBOYE has a BA from Yale University, an IPMA from Adonai University, and a Master's in Business Administration (MBA) from the University of Salford, Manchester.

He was born in South Africa but is presently based in Nigeria as a motivational speaker and marriage counselor in institutions, sectors, and seminars with young and upcoming managers all over Africa.

Acknowledgments

I want to express my sincere gratitude to everyone who helped with the "FAQ on Communication in Marriage." Their encouragement, insight, and support have been priceless throughout this journey.

I want to start by acknowledging the fact that, without God, this guide wouldn't have been possibly achieved.

And also, to my spouse, who has always been motivating and supportive in making this task successful, I will always love and appreciate you.

I have many couples to appreciate who have shared their experiences, challenges, and victories with me over the years. Your openness, weakness, and tenacity have enhanced the book's pages and provided priceless insights into the difficulties of marriage communication.

My earnest gratitude goes to my family and friends for their continuous support and encouragement during this journey. Your wise advice, tolerance, and words of support have helped me get through the complicated process of writing and releasing this book.

I sincerely thank the specialists and experts who kindly offered their knowledge and skills in marriage and communication. Your advice and thoughts have improved this book's quality and depth, and I appreciate your contributions.

Finally, I would like to express my profound gratitude to all of the readers of this work. As you journey through the communication process in your marriage, I hope that the knowledge, direction, and encouragement provided within these pages will inspire and empower you.

I sincerely appreciate your help.